Gerry Potter's L

Photo by Paul Neads

Gerry Potter is a poet, playwright, actor, director, and both creator and destroyer of the infamous gingham diva Chloe Poems. National Museums Liverpool lists him amongst their city's leading LGBTQIA+ icons, and he was profiled in the documentary film *My Name is Gerry Potter*, which premiered at Homotopia. His first collection of domestic/fantastic theatre-verse, *Planet Young*, was Bafta-winner Sophie Willan's book of choice on BBC TV's *Between the Covers*.

★ As *Chloe Poems*

Published by •The Bad Press, ■Route
◆ First published by Mucusart, re-issued by Flapjack Press

GERRY POTTER'S
Li'l Book o' small Poems
(or is it?)

Flapjack Press

flapjackpress.co.uk

Exploring the synergy between performance and the page

Published in 2023 by Flapjack Press
Salford, Gtr Manchester
⊕ flapjackpress.co.uk f Flapjack Press
🐦 FlapjackPress ▶ Flapjack Press

ISBN 978-1-7396231-0-4

Cover by Brink

Printed by Imprint Digital
Exeter, Devon
⊕ digital.imprint.co.uk

A UNESCO City
of Literature

Complex Post-Traumatic Stress Disorder

For years I've been plagued by depression/anxiety/insomnia. Like most sufferers, I've found a way of haphazardly coping, and although sometimes mentally/physically debilitating, that's all I thought it was.

Three years ago, I was diagnosed with c-PTSD [Google it], blowing my tiny mind wide open. Not necessarily size/weight of said diagnosis, but after two-and-a-half years of psychotherapy I realised it wasn't just depression/anxiety/insomnia, and I'd indeed lived a young life of extended trauma. Didn't particularly want such a prognosis, but part of me welcomed it; more importantly, the nature of it being explained. It lifts lids on so much, not just my bonkers life trajectory, but the work. The chopping/strobing surrealistic imagery oft' employed isn't glib me creatively riffing off-the-cuff, it's how my head naturally/ unnaturally churns; what my over-thinking brain has, for nearly six decades, been repetitively spinning.

This book isn't all about c-PTSD, but like everything I've done is holistically engined by it, and by me coming to terms with a head seeing largely in tormenting, off/on, filmic blasts. I used to be concerned about the eccentrically aesthetic oddness of that chaotically-disjointed imagery. Not anymore. For example, in 'A Small Poem About Being Hawk', I now completely understand why I'm able to relate gliding on mountainous updrafts to being a just-plinked, spinning, tiddlywink counter.

My next book, *6A Blackstock Gardens*, will detail the origins of my mental health conditions – and a whole lot more; an auto-biographical account of my emotionally turbulent first eight years on this huge planet of ours. No poetry, just straightforward prose. But it'll be life-lived 'n' informed c-PTSD prose.

Much love to you, especially friends. I know at times I've been more than a li'l bit of a big handful.

Contents

Foreword

Manchester's Greenroom, 2009.

The open mic poetry night Freed Up is in full swing. Its hosts Dominic Berry and Steve O'Connor take turns to introduce the poets and perform a poem or two of their own.

I'm a new face; an infant on the scene, watching in awe as others use words in ways that I can't yet fathom. The total number of poems I have performed in front of an audience stands at 2.

Sat towards the front of the stage, by the window that is regularly used by drunk people to heckle the acts, sits a guy in his 40s – blue jeans, casual shirt, Adidas trainers, shaved head. There's a buzz around him. He seems popular, animated, very much at home in his surroundings.

When Dominic tells us that we're in for a treat and introduces him as "Gerry Potter", my immediate expectation is posh. I mean he has to be right, with a name like *Gerry Potter*?

After 14 years of sharing stages, poems and pints with him, that initial misguided attempt at poet profiling seems hilarious to me now. As Scouse as Scottie Road and the perfect antidote to posh – Gerry showed me that night (and pretty much every time he's opened his gob since) what poetic spark looks like; what it means to mean every word and cherish every syllable; what it is to truly get what words can do and (one of the reasons we get on so well) to fully appreciate the release that comes from connecting with an audience poetically. When I talk about release, I mean from the pressures of past trauma. I'm talking about parachuting into our past and hoping we don't land on spiked railings – so that we can celebrate the characters who live on in our minds unchanged, unflappable, unharmed. So that we can echo the sounds of laughter and adventure that inhabit the derelict land-scapes of grief, and honour the memories that refuse to go quietly. There's power in that and in the sharing of it, and I don't know anyone better at turning it into poetic brilliance than Gerry Potter.

His poetry not only brings us to our feet, it escorts us to our car, draws our attention to the shine of the chassis, the gleam of the wheel rims, the plush interior, the calm caress of the music flowing through its speakers. But it could also pull up in a transit van, bundle us into the back, punch us in the gut and demand our full attention. It depends on the poem.

In the spirit of this book of small poems, here's a small one in honour of the man himself:

City street thinker.
Philosophical foot-fall.
Glimpsed in passer-by peripherals.
Today has written him...
Mission on a man.
Striding through the shadows
of the towers
his thoughts are loftier than.

David Viney

Introduction

Big and small, what do I actually mean by that? Never too sure to be perfectly honest. For example, I absolutely adore being dwarfed by nature and architecture. Plonk me anywhere near an Irish mountain or slap bang in the middle of New York, I'm happy as Larry. Although definitely diminutive, around those gigantic landmarks I don't feel in any way miniature; in fact, much more 'part of'. Am small, of course, but within the almost infinite confines of Carrauntoohil or the Chrysler Building I'm near camply colossal: a flurrying, bipedal, anxiously-informed, over-exclaiming, wide-eyed dot.

How piquantly petite am I though, if I not only see but thrill to height, perhaps viscerally honouring its sky-high vastness? That shit don't shrink too Alice to me, sugar. As humans we're kinda obsessed by height/size; an inbuilt, instinctive form of constantly measuring capitalism, more often than not wanting more... ask those greedy gays, we're always gaggin' for an extra couple o' inches.

Smaller we are, taller we are, more we see. At the bottom of a skyscraper, I see it all; atop [and on a clear day], a piffling/trifling me sees a bigger/broader everywhere else. Because we're human and having bally-well conceived the skyscraper, it gives us an intellectual, emotional, aesthetic dominance, and even if that concrete/steel/glass behemoth tragically earthquake crumbles, horrendously injuring, perhaps killing titchy/frail/unimportant us, it can only have epically, disaster movie collapsed cos we first-place put it there. Pretty much the same with once unnavigable mountain ranges and juddering cable cars; although metallically compact in cubist stature, we do always seem to find our ways around seriously bumpy mountainous terrains. Neither a gargantuan alp nor imposing skyscraper can do any of that. Just us, and then, let's cliff face it, only a select few.

I've neither been an architect nor cable car engineer, haven't those sizes of ambition or ideas, but could well be the same physical height of said architect/engineer, and if not, imagine I'm not that much bigger/smaller. Even if that same architect/engineer magically big Alices a whole foot taller, they're nowhere near the scale of Errigal or The Empire State Building. They may well be into poetry though – could even be good at it, perhaps reading/performing at many of the small open mic nights liberally peppered about our mythically big world.

At spoken word nights I've rubbed pissed-up poetic shoulders with people who've built oil rigs, rollercoasters, erected dams, tiny deep-sea divers first-hand witnessing the magnificent inky depth 'n' breadth of our outer-spacious oceans; those same extraordinary people doing/building/seeing ginormous external things, writing/presenting something innocuously internal as everyday observational poetry. I can't tell you just how much I've always thrilled to that. Poetry isn't inanimate like a mountain or a skyscraper and, because occasionally written by people who climb/design them, how malleably big does that make poetry? Does size matter, what is size and where does it go? Is poetry bigger than the tallest building, highest mountain, wider than our deepest ocean, faster than the most speeding of bullets? However it size/speed identifies, for me at least, the growing/shrinking jury will always be out on those perilously expanding questions.

My guess is everything's smaller/taller/faster/deeper all at the same time, including nature, towers, oceans, bullets and poetry. How big/small is the biggest/smallest poem? As big/small as them all, surely. How long's a piece of thinking, a haul of longing, a heal of learning? A one-bullet bang, *boom* you're a talling Alice down, and have always thought it best remembering wee Ben Nevis has absolutely no idea he's hefty Mount Everest's li'l brother.

Be it with crampons, elevators, quills, diving bells, guns or keypads, seems nearly all of us are trying to scale something, perhaps one day whilst climbing past the huddled, bone-frozen bodies of long dead ideas, maybe reaching some kind of personally uplifting, creatively summiting pinnacle. Who knows? Big/small, poetry doesn't – *these* poems; some about huge things one-page-sized or smaller, others about small things one-page-sized or taller.

Same goes for interpersonal relationships, how do they factually measure? I've hosts of enormous relationships under my copious life belt, but one of those relationships can, I suppose, disguise themselves smaller than some bigger others – or can it? I'm thinking of Paul Lerwill, then Rosetta Stones' Gregory Gray, eventually becoming the folksy/punky, MySpace/YouTube sensation, Mary Cigarettes. Now let's get this right, was Ms Cigarettes a huge internet singing sensation or is that just tiny me mulling impossible height? Gonna say here, if only li'l ol' me [which it's not], then yes, he/she was/is an immense series of digitally-inspiring, life-lived sensations.

Mary left our earthbound platform in 2019, but you can nevertheless World Wide Web conjure her – that filthy angel's still high as a kite 'n' sonically warbling up there in The Cloud. My main point being, I never once physically met Paul, Greg, or as I'd prefer to know him/her, Mary. Decades ago, when inhabiting The Gingham Diva Chloe Poems, Mary Cigarettes would on occasion [and always a pesky secretly] come to see Chloe perform, then excitably make contact on MySpace, telling me how much he'd enjoyed her performance [she particularly loved Chloe's epic poem 'The Effeminate']. It was just Mary's eccentric, personal way, soon becoming 'our' eccentric, personal way; we only ever communicated through social media. I'm long-guessing he was shielding me from the many conflicting enormities of her considerably substantial characters.

Saying all that, I consider Mary a big influence in/on my small life. Don't normally suffer crises of confidence and if do, seldom communicate them. Did with Mary though. One particularly tortuous night, in true keyboard worrier style, I frantically typed at her a pained/anguished artist's everything and suddenly, in this seemingly miniscule internet relationship, Mary was hugely, widely magnificent. I'll never forget that time or he/her. "I've too many poems about dancing, Mary!" "Feck off Gerry, y'can never have enough poems about dancing. We're gay men of a certain age, all we've ever done properly is dance, write more!" The deliciously complex Mary Cigarettes, only close friend never met I genuinely grieve for. He'd rebelliously revel in the poetically paradoxical size of that... warra gal!

Also recall my physically met dear friend/mentor Roger Hill [who wrote the Foreword to *Accidental Splendour of the Splash*] intently chatting with me about that book's thematic 'li'l splashes'. Short poems influenced by the formlessly fluid week-in/week-out, surrealist energies of our Everyman Youth Theatre improvisations, spilt straight from my head and with minimal editorial interference, instantly committed to the page. I'm remembering how intricately intrigued he was by them and how the size of that literary intimacy massively, positively impacted on me. "Gerry, what does *a cardigan of trees* actually mean?" That complex question simply being asked meant the world to me.

Although these big/small poems are instant li'l splashes, finely edited 'n' reshaped, they're from the same anarcho-improvisational pool. I even think a few of those original li'l splashes may have accidentally splish-sploshed their sneaky way into a much more edited here; wouldn't put it past the pernickety/surrealistic short-arsed blighters. That's small/big worlds for you, always colliding, smashing together to form something different, perhaps bigger/smaller collisions, littler/larger worlds... I sincerely hope so. All our blinkin' Wonderlands eh, tiny/tall, gathering archipelagos of the same ideas.

Right now, I'm orbiting high above planet Earth in a spaceship of my own essential making, looking down at our tiny, isolated blueberry, thinking... *li'l poems about big 'n' small, Gerry? Well, that really is about the size of it.*

Gerry Potter

Li'l Book o' small Poems

A Small Poem About Me

Sit bad,
really bad,
über-lounged,
doesn't help my round-shouldered posture.
Sit like reclining on a nineteen-fifties deckchair.

I type a structured anarchic,
not dissing rules,
sometimes mindfully respectful of rules,
but they don't pride-of-place, boasting prize-winning rosettes.
Rule's one log the fire.

I'm typing small poems in hope they commute,
shoulders and hips crowded,
my head a rush-hour tube.
All a bit London,
still a louche nineteen-fifties off-West End revue.

Sit bad,
really bad,
but never been one for comfort.

A Small Poem About Being An Insect

Elbows, knees and wall-crawling,
jutting out of an exoskeleton dig.
I've been spidering before
but never ant, nor God forbid, fly.

Clinging by pincer to avoid tumbling,
ideally ignoring sticky.
Unless honey,
unless so sweet, I sickly die.

Insect long legs don't suit suspenders.
Drag's for far too fleshy mammals
and their injured, desert plains screeching.

Once told a story,
read a book, saw theatre,
one chomp devoured a silk-cocooned moth,
sat dark through a movie about light,
every time and supposedly surreal,
understood.

On my back wriggling,
the world stands and not for first or last time
raises its boot.

A Small Poem About Size

Mountain me a snow-peaked scaled,
moon riding starscapes till space rips.
Deep in black holes,
even bigger versions of ourselves.

Been huge and tiny,
an all-over spill of *drink grow, drink shrink.*
Oops, that's me drunk and once again giving Alice
a scolded smalling for her money.
In a land of giants
we're soon too big for our little boots.

Know the tunnels, ate the soil,
swallowed a starburst's show-tuning signature.
From a mouth full of earthworms
another messy big bang of spat-out planets.

A Small Poem About The Do Of Don't

When we don't love we don't earth,
soak, root, drink;
when we don't love we don't power,
bask, reach, tall;
we don't open,
don't know what could be known.

When we don't love we don't know;
don't know bunch, grasp, bouquet, symphony,
gifting flower of apology.

We do when we don't love, do don't,
big don't and when we do big don't,
when not doing,
love smalls.

When we do big don't,
love don't bloom,
doesn't float, seed, travel breeze,
bruise y'knuckles, saucily rouge y'knees,
ease y'wheeze, hold back y'sneeze,
doesn't land,
grow.

A Small Poem About The Unheard

Your ego, mirror-climaxing, mega-splats,
hijacking the shit out of a spotlit splash.
In becalming of hairbrush comedowns,
you sigh-sky at dizzying heights.

We, The Unheard, are clam-closed in non-applauded shyness,
roadblocked and locked in.

Anarchy of imagination reopens slammed.
Draws spiral-patterned curtains and ambition's roaring
at four closing-in, too-ugly-wallpapered walls.

The posing superstar in us flouts,
denim'd, lamé'd, Paris-sequinned
and there's a light that's never not a full-lipped,
out-loud, slow pout.

Ablaze in eternity,
dreaming enormities of scorching belief.
Where The Unheard echo
in bedrooms of invisible choirs.

A Small Poem About Photographs

Time windows, mirror travelling,
looking, falling through,
monochromatism grabs me more.
Every sixties pub I've seen stilled,
inebriate hinterlands revisited.

Within them, breathing the seventies,
weight of its ashtrays, bottle of its ale,
sensing balladeering lament of glorious swansong.

Adore portraiture,
blemishless skin of wistful mothers,
how pearls emboldened and near Hollywood they look.

A Small Poem About Crumbs

Empty garden, lost key,
secrets kept and thrown away.
In bloated exotica of plumage,
full-throated call of blood-sound.

You're near me in recall,
unseen and breeze-shook.
I look to leaves' night-scented vibrato of visitation.

There's Hansel, there's Gretel,
curse of winter,
kiss of spring and on paths of memory,
crumbs.

A Small Poem About Remembering

Pavement hit but softer,
I land, moment-stutter then gone.
Sometimes scent,
almost always noise.

Another hop, thump-judder
and nearly able of touch.
Chalk numbers, trapped by squares
are ghosts 'n' scribbles shaped.

Pitch a stone.

Seven.

A Small Poem About Fireworks

On November 6th I'd delight at dead fireworks,
no narrative, without literature,
wasn't read or taught.
Whatever our strange relationship it was real,
mine,
ours,
poignant.

Maybe you had to have done it,
been that kid picking up.
Loved burnt-out rockets,
their scorched, broken sticks;
not sure how, felt like reward.

Those flaming colours,
a community collectively roaring,
all of us fire.
Next day's rain, remnants of old burning,
scents of smouldering,
over,
done,
gone.

Less than twenty-four hours,
half a night, half a day,
a tonne of minutes and centuries passed.

A Small Poem About City Centres

Back-handed, snuff-sniffing old dears, pub-cut pork pies.
Back-alley, cellar-clubbing and flirty dancing.
Knee-trembling in rat-scurrying entries and dirty gobbling.
Conjuring sepia scents of brethren belonging.
My city senses are spot on.

Find it hard to breathe, not pollution,
time's rushing to who knows where or why.
No interest in career minutiae
or why achievement supposedly matters.
I have opinions.

1977 and a barrer boy on Cases Street,
watching mornings pan out,
street cleaners, drunks 'n' punks.

Rusts haze, growing,
shops opening sing their own kind of music.
Love fashion's tatters,
loading barrers, obligatory safety-pins,
string-vested, mohair'd, piercings.

Sinking in, soaking up,
pile high patterning half-blackened bananas.
Being taught to hide bruises is intimate.

Pavement becomes me,
whole swallowed.

A Small Poem About Otherness

Glory be to the glorious roar,
to whyever originally there,
whenever crafted by whoever
and whatever it was ever supposedly for.

Understanding's a dodgy thoroughfare,
socialisation keys but never doors.
Peeping Toms lurked behind its creak
long before there were holes in walls.

Perhaps a belt of cosmic knowledge
you must be broken to receive.
Shut down, left out, battered around,
ragamuffin-scuffed about the knees.

Perhaps a song not known,
lowly lilting on baritonal breeze.
Feel its rumbling on shifting beds,
on bottomless rocks of rolling seas.

Ran from safeness failing me,
jumped from tightropes without nets.
Landing but not landing into
chaotically repetitive splats of otherness.

A Small Poem About The Past

I am old,
not young,
not eighteen trapped in fifty-nine.

Without Zimmer (for now),
own teeth (for now),
can boogie with the best (for now).
But I'm old, not young,
not a teenageing psychobilly pogoing in an old raver's body.

Here's to the future of course,
but y'should see my past.
I'm old,
was young,
am still ageing (for now)
and so completely proud of that.

A Small Poem About Youth

You get one long go, yet not long enough.
What you don't know, well, that can fuck right off.
The spin when dancing, a twisting, dynamite Schwarzkopf.
And we hysterically howl as eternals.

Of course you've cares, but now you've the world.
Waves of ribboning banners unfurled.
One of the boys, both, whatever, or one of the girls.
And we reach for stars in our pockets.

A Small Poem About Brad Davis

1979, Everyman Youth Theatre and it was so many things.
Maybe you find yourself properly once,
know I did; so much so, never had to search again.

Improvisation and Rocky Horror,
all things around and in-between,
our parties, a house-bounding legendary.
You get one throw of that kind of youth,
six of the dice.

So many images, teaching in every breath,
and our November trip to the cinema.
Knew John Hurt, he'd been Quentin Crisp,
Caligula even, but had never seen you.

Brad, you didn't make me gay,
but soon became my great dark jock.
Some bloke in a shower tried to kiss,
you rape-wanked over the window.

Can still hear the music, Vangelis,
those churning synths and that walk out the flicks,
alive with a pants-sized, growing knowing.

A Small Poem About 1981

Bombed-out on air atomised,
pathways invisible lead to pathways invisible
and synth-held together by safety pins.

Mustachio'd are leather-studded,
poppers-snorting and sweat-headed.
Songs anti-sung belted are cacophonous soaring,
emotion colds, emotion hots,
emotion's roaring for Friday's just-cashed Giro.
Hit 'n' run lovers,
kiss 'n' tellin' winners 'n' losers.

My heart knows itself,
other hearts know themselves,
off-headed hearts thump toilet oral.
Our hearts leap a guttersnipe diamanté,
are homemade bejewelled,
crafted from societally imposed self-loathing
and nineteen seventies anarchy.

Our hearts will soon be beating plague.

Once again, in cellars Aladdin and shadow shone,
my forty thieves and I, dancing.

A Small Poem About Unserious Poseurs

My memories are sharp-elbowed,
am fluent in pouting.
Eyes narrowing a side-slide and in enigmatic videos,
pretend starring.
Synthesisers are marrow'd sound,
blood deep in corpuscle of bone,
rising drones in long-dug earth,
a mythically pounding undergrounded.

Apparently everything was closing dark,
decaying industry dominating,
but from dancefloors, catching flirt of eyes,
it was waspishly arch, over-sexed, posed
and Babylon Hollywooding.

I'm lit up in palaces, opulent expanses,
ballroom'd-in with diesel dykes and pool tables.
Old queens wearying well-earned crowns,
names rearranged to garland their sissy.

Futurists tower, punks meticulous-studded,
romantics cheekbone, goths amphetamine and lager.
Time thick, loops a hesitant translucent,
zones are sepia-smoked and stepped upon.
Seriously unserious poseurs ghost-written by Wilde,
amber'd taverns, repeating.

Insurrections of choice, unwritten but chiselled,
never obeying, far more than ten,
entombed, completely dolled-up and commanding,
we keep taking the tablets.

Yeah, suggesting it Biblical because a cheeky milliner'd tilted,
Biblical's style.

A Small Poem About The Universe

Sprawl palleting into colours kiss,
hope lights hearts heavenly.

Not distracted by anything,
whatever else there is, wherever located,
there isn't more than this.

On beats and inbetweening,
moving amongst tears dried,
everyone's licking their own remarkable starburst.

In disco, we beautiful,
in bopping bass, rioting laughter sweats.

Thirty genies smoke-hiss,
dirtying a long haul down,
weaving through rhythm and what the universe knows.

A Small Poem About Time And Time Again

Happiest in the moment, eyeliner of storm,
no plan, no rehearsal,
wig plonked on the head of happening,
lippy drag, hips syncing.

Happiest letting control trip-slip
within accidents of dance, spinning.
Don't care how I get there,
what it takes or what I've taken to not care.
It alives, it alives,
hysterically creatures and Colin Clives,
a stitched-up sense of forever.
We are the 'we are' of time,
to times we were, to time connecting.

We travel;
I am tumble and fight,
humble and always right.

We love,
hurtle 'n' spill, pop 'n' pill,
lamplight swingin' a cheap thrill.

I've sat sky-side with gods and kite high,
giggle-bitched those unthinking non-believers.

A Small Poem About Mirrorballs

Swear dust's raving,
sheer dotted specks in corridor'd beam.
Skimming through strobes and once again bouncing off
spherical, nonsensical intensities of mirrorballs.

Swear we're dust,
swear I see us,
corridor'd,
hands air'd because we've always cared.

Staring beyond dotted dusts dancing in corridor'd beams,
split, re-split by strobing,
bouncing off spherical nonsensical intensities of mirrorballs.

A Small Poem About Escape

Something of a runner, always have been,
from things known and not.
My guess is running defines me;
we're who we are because?

It's always been sound,
roar the merrier;
I'm a bugger for making silence scream.
Being related to the dead,
you have to.

So, I run, some of it adventuring,
manic slews of aesthetic dancing.
Always noise though; addicted, I suppose.
I'm from Liverpool, we really dig it there…
noise is sound, *la*.

A Small Poem About Great Space

Colours run and in lakes of radiant ripple,
dreams blur.
In speckle-code,
tree-framed flashes of dawn and y'know,
somewhere scratching,
there's an idea.

In this space we create things,
a great space,
it's Queer.

Moon shot an overhead bright,
starscapes sparkling the big one
and spiralling comes easy-peasy shine.
Someone special once told me something and now,
I cherish all stories.

In this space we elevate things,
a great space,
it's Queer.

A Small Poem About Zhuzh

Electrica,
sizzlin', abundant and sparking,
another perfect move from those spot-on muthas.

Sun's firing a hallucinogenic eclipse,
cascading lips on cascading lips
and whispering hysterically,
we belt it out.

You got it like we all have,
a galloping, gossiping tuneful,
beautifully beastly and haphazardly side-saddle.
We're smashing down ruby hooves,
stomping out our age,
clubland cantering a performative display.

Circus carolling cacophony's chorus,
fun-powder flare and boom.

Imagine being the blast.

A Small Poem About Cocaine

Splice 'em up, line 'em out,
those emaciated Fosse hoofers
are streaky-powdered, shark-sneering
and arse-to-ground choppin' out the jazz.

Moments are targeting,
an arrow-headed diamond sharp,
zero's bullseye
as we fly into the storm lit.
Enlightening hitting, flash 'n' snow-torn,
night's strobing blizzarding and we're lost,
hoovering up mirrored constellations of The Plough.

Ice man cometh in mouths of other ice men,
crème de la ice screaming.
Addiction's sly sheening,
bubble-butt'd, landsliding,
handclapping a harsh-buzzed nose-bleeding.

A Small Poem About The Soul Cleansers

Could Eve it,
lift from ribs; Adam it in cool running water,
let ripples sheen a generous shimmer,
let starlight replenish and reshine.

Was told, *dream it spotlit, Gerry,*
and long taught not to be afraid of witches.
I know the role of the grubby cunning,
those rugged, ragged, salve dampeners.
They mucky-pup about the gills putting out moments
like you might a night-time's expecting cat.

Great movers, sift in and around moon bathing.
Boneless, rhythmical, touch air, sound soaking,
yes sir, they can boogie.
Gentlemen (especially the gay ones), they groove for you.
Thrown shapes catch your flight,
letting you in, welcoming you home.

Soul Cleansers clean up The Shiver,
the crone, the tramp, Dickens-hobble around demons
and hips bumping, borrow horns.

A Small Poem About The Shiver

Drunken, drugged-up homeless see it,
heroine, Fentanyl and acid are keys.
Prayer-bowed women
and loved-up ravers' vibrations are linked.
It may well be God's hand swinging The Rattle.

Passing through and into,
licking colour, massage of light.
I've stepped onto metropolises of nowhere,
cityscape liquid and pavement song.

So off my head once, a gay man running didn't stop
and passed right through me.

A Small Poem About Drum Punch

Beats of booze, kickin'-in of drugs,
speed snares 'n' clapping snaps,
trapped in back feet's and fast feats of boom-bam-blast.

Rope lit 'n' rough hung, songs blue sung,
two wrungs do make rights,
light ladders trailblaze a smoke haze,
we're glazed-eyed within tight-thigh'd fist fights.

Disco blood,
bobbing hoody, would if y'could,
split sounds understood,
where there's willies there's ways,
gays,
blue-jean'd 'n' waylaid,
some days you can't wait to bomb.
"When you wanna cum!"

Scrum of it strums the big one and there you are,
gone.
You've hit the wavelength,
from strength to quiver a silvering simmering sliver,
quantum lighting The Void still surfing The Shiver.

A Small Poem About AIDS

We read, *only Americans*,
laughed, thinking it a right-wing Christian lie.
Danced laughing, ridiculous,
no disease can kill just gay men.

Before it landed and everything was new,
all of us in it,
cellar club submerged within theatre and disco.

When you discover freedom,
strobing Donna summits of joy,
nothing can touch or hurt anymore.
Brian and I ruled those dancefloors;
shimmying through high notes, we'd neon.

Damn lucky to be part of,
just before it hit.
Not knowing its shadow
meant we didn't know its shadow.

Colin, Vinnie.
Wasn't only Americans.

A Small Poem About Good People

There's lots of them y'know,
brewing up 'n' brushing away.
Helpers without ego
(well, maybe a little),
without reward
(well, maybe some).

Blood-givers,
pouring out all there is to share.
Always remember
there are good people everywhere.

A Small Poem About Hangovers

Front of my head's jig-aching,
it's all about a too-full noise.
Blasts of eternity are boogie-knotted,
still eternally romancing.

Last night Caleb 'n' I proper popper'd-up,
slut-dropped an E mimic-quipping in time.

My cracked pavement gays get this,
their traumas glitter it disco.
So much so, pain's worth it,
deserved even.

Yeah, a windswept wiped out,
part of me strobing multicoloured blackouts.
But it can get frenetically busy in here,
so this hangover's a gift;
believe when I say, density lifts.

Minds like mine respect exhaustion.

A Small Poem About Those Whispers

Want to rediscover that liberating darkness,
nights out forever written about.
I've bumped with vampires, snorted beak with lycanthropes;
oh those darling monstrous fools,
thirst-game squirming with boogying ghouls.
It's in the whispers, those whispers,
ones you hear between here and The Shiver.

Soft hisses of hot hits 'n' sneer misses,
stolen kisses from thieving lips.
Want to rediscover those ne'er-do-wells,
sit on soul-sold carousels of spinning lives.
Sex bought, sex gels;
in dishonourable disco,
sordid thrives.

I want what's no longer there.

It's in the whispers, those whispers,
ones you hear between thumping air.
Those whispers bought, those whispers sold,
ones whispering between young and old.

A Small Poem About Now

Point to but can't see,
future elicits opaque responses,
more about placing than placed.

Can point to and see the past,
misshape its repetitive bruising.
Not all black or blued,
occasionally purple.
Skin, paper, screen are surfaces aimlessly,
blamelessly written on.

Now, a crossroads sign,
creak-twisting in wind.
Now's a tale-telling, wood-worming, gnaw,
more murdered mystery than cartoon.

I hear now, dying, gnawing.

A Small Poem About Turning Sixty

Once wrote a book called *Fifty*,
as decades go, went far too quickly,
wish it'd graced, favoured a li'l more slickly,
had me loosely elsewhere and a tiny bit sickly.

Thought thoughts and they sped so fastly,
some thoughts spat a gruelling ghastly.
Dreams of teen nostalgia wobble unsteadfastly,
lip-licking chomps of a Sayers' pasty.

A loved life of improvisational madness,
liberally peppered by assaulting sadness.
In amongst good, monstering badness
and darting ovations of glittering fabness.

A Small Poem About Old Nose

Soggy-fat, like a wet lump of clay,
see it in reflection and smile.
It's long-johns 'n' grandad-shaped and glows a warning.

Gerard, you've an old nose now.

A Small Poem About Double Chins

Within ageing it aches face,
from mirror's top looking to drop.

Aquiline flirts of taut skin
vainly hope in folds there's wisdom
and not yet another chin.

A Small Poem About Charles Hawtrey

Sharp as a dart, pinched as a shrew,
I've a feeling no one knew you better than you.
Multi-talented trickster,
limp-wristed mister,
Little Miss Sinister if needs be.
Trolling those sailors,
be they Her Majesty's or filthy whalers,
never letting society's failures limit you.

Fractiously talented top bill bitch,
narcissistically multi-faceted,
izzywizzylet'sgetshowbizzy witch.

My too-skinny godhead,
giving loads of public bog head,
no one knows the gladiatorial guts you bled
over those plush, flush lavatorial scenes.

High priestess of glittery theatre queens,
not one of those pithily glowering unseens,
legacy gleaming in glasses of treble vodka and hits.
Shining star in my eyes
with drag's slightly more flattering smaller tits.

Your pissed-up, kissed-up hissy fits
and those Carry On chortling *oh hello* highs.

A Small Poem About Happening Bedlams

Once asked to describe a rose: *Exquisite carnage,* I replied.
Drop-jawed, my inquisitor nodded then asked: *Why carnage?*
I said: *That's nature, serendipitous accident in Cinemascope,*
widescreen and mountain-ranged, a happening bedlam;
ask any gay cowboy.

We talked around the brutality of flowers,
how jaggedly spiked,
prickly stinging slasher movies.
Their longevity's eternally brief,
how like in *Psycho* beauty's a huge but tiny part.
Lilies are roses in drag.

A pissed-up conversation,
unafraid of language,
of testing it out or getting it wrong.
Our laughter raucously littered
with serial killing cross-dressed thorns.

A Small Poem About Rain

Air change, re-breathe,
inhalation's a clouded *splish*.
Tongue senses soil and licking clods of when,
we are.

Weighs on you, not necessarily heavily
but not light, neither drizzle nor splash.
Aged centuries spill a billion downpours.

Just went the chippy;
face alive and soaked in autumn,
visited another world.
I see for miles through mizzle,
it's easy.

Big on mists, how they comfort and portent.
The body's witcheries are solace.
Moments you God-catch.

Guess I dig a soggy gig,
how it slide-sways in,
plummets, drenches and drowns.

I'm earth, therefore must be moon.

A Small Poem About Being Water

Sea's in powdered form, jabbing,
spittle-punches drench, splatter-sting,
they sharp attack and in seconds,
blanket.
With only soaked skin for company,
the shop-bought silks of cling.

Could Manchester you,
let's face it, every fucker does,
but you squall worldwide storms.

Love dampened caresses,
moist lips invisible kissing.
We are relationship,
with or without you our bodies are water.

A Small Poem About A Storm

In progressions of a millionth of a second,
portal'd and window shopping,
gifts for deities go boom.

These are how your gardens grow,
so many ways of splitting a sycamore.
Are berries blood-spots,
facsimile dotted throughout family trees?
Are there doors within doors opening and shut off?

Heaven's good 'n' grieving.
Tears plod weighty, blot and sandbag.

Walls taste of whispers.
These paths glow.

Crazy paving's multi-freckling like red heads in summer.

A Small Poem About Heatwaves

Sandbagged and hot water soaked,
heavy leaden.
Too hot's a bit like grief if grief wasn't loss
but dead weight draining.
A similar density to, but no laid-out body,
no over-emotive eulogy,
no lover's ring encircling third-fingered familial misery.

The planet's atop me,
suffocating, but some breath.
Maybe more wet pillow pressed down by a murderous nanny,
expertly played by Davis – and she's flammable Method,
going for it.
An Oscar worthy performance;
Bette's on fire.

Paradoxically more winter-bowled porridge,
coagulated salty.
An unattractive lumpen,
piping hot, thick to stir.

A Small Poem About Late Summer

My guess, their heads turn like mine,
can see tawnying before its time.
I've ancestral links with our cunning,
salve-bubblin' crones on first name terms with roots.

Within dusk, no one night's the same,
unique's a way of fingerprinting.
Being on right-minded worms with earth's the bomb.

Streams sing, sun blesses,
they're out there tree-souling
and horizons aren't meant for fingering.

A Small Poem About February

Damp's a way of clawing,
diggers falling into earths of you,
sky's grey roaring,
auld sniggers trawling around dearth's of you.

Mourning's like this,
leave us cantankerous heaped,
bereave us crumbling,
side-road huddled 'n' tumbling.

Trees preparing promise look scribbled by children:
terminally bored children with little thought left.
The ones refusing to play, colour or rhyme.

Walking, pencil-sketched by sharpened sighs,
on the off-chance, mumbling.

A Small Poem About Thinking Days

When skies colour a hectic multi,
a spread of sprawling hues,
I feign cloud-blanket and fly.

On thinking days, I'm covered,
even if it's the Blues.
Sometimes pain is song,
need words: words sing.
Why I write.

Over-cranking a mournful mull,
lost in dreaming;
on thinking days quiet's frantically screaming
a Blues fuckin' murder.

Alone's spelling my name and missing out the G.
Dangerously thin-iced, skating on cracking misery.
That's the thing with thinking days: their nightmares,
failing hierarchies and hallucinogenic inefficiencies,
they're creatively compulsory.

Guess I'm good at The Void,
on thinking days we kinda marry.
Ring on third, left hand,
The Void, finger and 'erry.

A Small Poem About The Sky

A derelict docklands,
busy with haunts of full employment:
my safe place.

Space and waste,
curious scent of salt wood,
decomposing decoration of decay.
At home with the rotting splintered,
it cosy-deeps and blankets.

With history behind you,
sky opens a flowering optimistic,
clouds and pinks wide smile,
determined blues welcome, comfort.

No distance, no hierarchy,
just warming realisations of breadth and life.

Remember once,
one of those well-thumbed story-told days,
beguiling, muddle and end...
sky colouring me immortal.

A Small Poem About River Wolves

Tracksuit'd and trainer-paw'd he prowls,
a water walking light foot.
Pads rippling a circular direction,
scents salt 'n' docks.
Half-eyed stare,
sun's dusking, shine's melting.
Mersey's sinking a sozzled goodbye and steaming,
she sings.

Whistle howl his calling card
and full moon blooms hello.

A Small Poem About Lost

Discovered found because of lost,
lost bullies invisible.
Over where directionless is signposted,
unseen tinying a distancing dot

Maps of snakes no ladders,
games unwinnable,
scaly-slipping,
kin shed and rattled.

Under sand, weighted world,
treasureless buried,
just you and the hermitting conches.

Stick a pin in;
stab a hole and here you are,
marking the spot,
topographically speared in design.

A Small Poem About Twisting

In aftermaths of everybody's everything,
all whatevers weave and forever fleetingly lingers.

Somewhere a child's barely surviving;
looks to freedom of sky,
searches for flocked togethering.
She's old man's fingers
and, carefully circling them around clouds,
makes shapes.

Imagines starlings' pattern,
remembers song, mother singing.
Kneading fruitless plain flour scones and wanting to be
Princess Pretty of the chipped porcelain plate.

Other thoughts misplaced,
strewn,
a brothel Tarot sold to futures forgotten.
Tower tumbles,
lightning strikes
and Death Nell collects her wailing fallen.

A bony finger's hovering.
Circles.
Twist?
Turned an up 'n' over edgy,
the bleakest card,
a princess fruitlessly baking plain flour scones.

A Small Poem About A Routine Slowed

On parquet, shrill 'n' bent-kneed,
his secret identity screamed... *Walls know nothing!*
The mirror gnawed, rhythm ripped his skin
beating it back to Blues.
In reflection bar'd, his ballet ghosts.

Crawling under decks, sounds of slide cross over.
Neon snails slime a sluggish routine,
are mud-paced Rumba'n
a sin-stinkin' cha-cha-cha.

Crowd burst, torrenting steps,
tormenting bents are raving in rain.
Insane and connecting in waving,
they're spotted, acid-dappled and storm-jigged.

The thundered clap,
him and his just-found applause Grindr shelter.

Over mountainous motel they came,
in his face, all over his balls.

A Small Poem About Full English

Repetitively mumbles, uneven banal stuff like...
Toast tastes funny wi' tea an' have y'noticed when dunkin',
oily residue left on't surface of brew?
Never quite sure anything makes sense.
A terror of risk-taking conversation.
Avoids avoiding.

Can't ask for toilet roll.
Hell-bent on bodily functioning secrets.
Has never convinced with *hello*.

Envies relationships but can't have one;
they're something others evoke to haunt time.

Today's Thursday, special treat day:
full English breakfast in a tin.

A Small Poem About Barley And Blood

Souped veins clog 'n' gloop,
sludging bad fats of his body pot.
Rivers of purée thickened by age,
added to rage,
today he's a too-stirred, unflavoured sage.

Barley and blood, barely alive,
a soupçon of all he once was.
A long-brewed broth,
playing dodge-the-wife Saturday five-a-side.

Diced, drained, sieved,
ladled by labels he buys too-tight jeans,
leeks, lamb and yellow sticker'd asparagus.
A cock-a-leekie, consommé, colander guy;
seen better displays,
bought cheaper bargains.

Dreams of oxtail still attached to its bull,
in changing room toilets, a sly ham shank.

A Small Poem About Being Coupled With...

Veiled but not y'marrying kind,
holster's hangin' a confetti-filled shotgun.
All I know about union a child could engrave
on the side of a bullet.
Guess I'm flesh piercing,
bang,
but outside of blast,
blank.

Orbit targets, afraid to land,
I'll embed but it's all far too long;
with or without me it's bigger within you.

Lined up with other ammunition,
ignore communication,
leave repetitive machining for dancefloors.
Silver-shelled not gold-ringed,
I know what my right hand's for.

Smack my arsenal, still here,
behind, slack of the queue.
On the back pot-boiler,
shot at and wide o' the mark bullseyed.
Russian rouletting, propose begging for mercy,
booty-boom-boom on one knee, trembling.

Going down but not out,
a be-glittered Madonna hat hangs bevvied on my altar.

A Small Poem About Love

No doubt of its existence,
know it personally,
sent it sexy texts.
But it's a dodgy bastard love,
bit of a spiv.

Always feel it's slyboots selling something,
brown paper packaged, under the table.
Seen it passed around pubs
with the knock-off aftershave and meat raffle.

A part of me wants but doesn't wholly trust,
but do see it in moments.
I've loved a good few one-night stands,
loved strangers, danced.

Not completely sold on companionable bonding;
I've touched it,
a trustworthy untrustworthy...
bit of a spiv.

A Small Poem About Song

My guess is we know them all,
buried beat and lyricism.
In tongues tied and in other places,
I dance from my soul.

Thoughts waft melodiously,
half-cut 'n' full sung;
there are basketfuls tisketing, tasketing,
three blags culling.
My guess is we crow-cloak them all.

Don't just give it to love,
jealousy begs to disagree,
iridescence purples a Poe-feathered murderously.

We know evil sings.

A Small Poem About People

I'll never forget her face,
such tale-telling brutal contortion.
The twisting ache of apology,
never seen eyes sadder.

Tried to roll the toy car back to the toddler,
it veered under a chair.
The toddler cried,
its mother told her it was okay.
She sat back, defeated,
life losing,
weight of loss palpable.

Wanted to hug her 'n' maybe would have
if we weren't in A&E.

A Small Poem About Soul Fool

Soul Fool rolls down and falls up moods,
flipping big within crippling anxiety spirals.
Soul Fool's done and looking for easy ways out,
both ways,
always.

Y'gotta give it to Soul Fool,
they'll take it all night then bolt,
never faster than when running away.
Soul Fool locomotives, makes commotion,
is it a bird, is it a plane?
Everybody's doin' the brand new Soul Fool.

Flare cape 'n' sly glide,
superhero hand-jiving the sand slide.
Soul Fool ain't got no X-ray vision,
wall's a wall unless prison.

A Small Poem About Hawk

Imitating flight, I've paintbrush fingers,
a day dressing artist didn't give the game away
and am giddily sat, tiddlywink thinking.

I plink in tiddlywink so perhaps I hawk,
squark adorable plonk and giggle,
minutia flipping counter cults of youth power.
Look to roofs and how slates slide,
everything angles.

Pressed on and occasionally potted.
Over theres of everything and its rivering streams.
With compendium as companion,
mimic game 'n' glide.

A Small Poem About The Isle Of Arran

Nothing's vividly overspent or über-bright gaudy,
just muted hazes of fades-blended story.
Hits of softness night scent, cushioning dreams.

Sea, soul-searing compassionate,
sea, nonchalantly scheming.
Blue-green turquoise dusks and tall on an island saving,
my handsome lighthouse rocks.

A Small Poem About Joan Crawford

Hollywood-wired and we hung on every word,
even in *Trog* you struck a pre-hysterical chord.
Let's face it baby, no guy kissed like Gable
and a too-highly-strung Johnny Guitar'd.

Ambition driven, come-to-bed-eyed,
flapping out a frenzied Charleston.
Frill shook on pussy power,
dry gin bitchin' out the witchin' hour.
Noir Mildred silhouette and pistol packin'
an unmarried point-blank shotgun.

Driven maddened because car crashed,
life like yours an abusive pile.
Swirling around sewerage of Lucille LeSueur,
of course you slavishly craved a Draino'd floor.

Queen of Movies and hatchet girl,
fight royally packing a punch.
Choppin' out lines, machete,
poppin' pills a medicine'd confetti.
Jane got it half right...
but'cha Joan, y'are on that throne.

I don't think the public does know what that Oscar means...
but I know you did.

A Small Poem About The Gays

Lava's bubbling a smouldering unseen,
love's thundergrounded hot 'n' sizzling,
searching for rocks to pour through and gush.
Bare, perfectly sculpted, fur-chested eruptions
look so fuckable in bleached-out 501s.

In Utrecht and he was a DJ, a god,
face masculine, gentle.
Brian fell in, love at first sight,
told me: *He's the handsomest ever!*

Never a more natural blond,
when looking, you blue-eye rocketed,
his English the most sexually charged pidgin
and that packet, oh Jesus God, don't get me started.

Men aren't like buses,
you can wait for ages and they don't all cum at once.

We took a strawberry, first time hearing techno,
canal-side trees multicoloured flowering.
Tonight's volcanoes are spunking blossom.

A Small Poem About The Krays

Both bent as nine bob notes
but the gays don't onside you.
Perhaps it's a class thing or maybe we don't like
calculating, psychotic, serial killers.

We love our mums though,
every one a well-turned-out matriarch.
Archetypal pearly queens,
shiny-white sequining our duchesses.

Both of you, glamorous, dangerous;
we're meant to be turned on by that.
Best buddy'd with Babs,
stood mythically centurion around Judy.

Vauxhall 1995, Brian's just died,
sat in a pub and overheard a loud gay say
he must have infected more guys than he knows.
Just before combination therapies and his table
erupts with shrieking maniacal laughter.

We don't let you in though,
maybe you just weren't gay enough,
or perhaps that calculating, psychotic, serial killer thing.

A Small Poem About Writing

Head wrecked,
I'm a billion beaks pen-pecked.
One word houses other story,
every entry,
large world,
tale minutiae,
verbal diary.

Wish it just a quick, sleek, signature,
flash-scribbled and ready.
A Barbara Cartland rocksteady!
Wish there a wish able to finish it.

Excavation cold seams,
more dead canaries than gold.

A Small Poem About Ladybird Books

Not sure what came first, Catholicism or Rumpelstiltskin,
either way they chaotically blurred.
Pictures masquerading as words,
too much for a young soul, maybe?

Deep reds, velvet blues,
fuzzy material, smooth page.
Words braid rope-plaited ponytails,
long yarn, thick with manipulative adventure.
Handsome Princes bored me,
running with colours, the buzz.

I saw seven dwarfs in St. Gerard's stained glass,
St. Gerard kissing Snow White under Santa Claus.
Happy ever after, pillars of salt,
ran the sermon and narrative.

Felt like diving into a public baths-full of images,
a municipal oil on water of panoramic splash.
Never once clocked Jesus,
but sure as Hell blimped Satan in those Ladybirds.

A Small Poem About The Rot In The Hearth

Colour of old pages,
where stories leap and land,
heaviness of print,
slight reliefs of words, thick ink rope ladders.
Didn't we climb down into picture books,
make them dens?
Remember weaving escape from imagination?

You can't see the rot in the hearth.
Back to it,
arse rubbing 'n' warming is when it shows face.
I'd use a particular ash as colouring,
scrape scratched across paper you'd score
a subtle mottled grey.

We were all about fire, made us feel older.
There where images, stories, and on good days,
words.

I recall first un-watching and how it let me down.
A bloodshot cyclopean eye,
staring.

A Small Poem About Body-Bagged Ego

Flesh bordellos pump,
raising a rough gliding paid stab.
Barely bares, think about it, a lone nipple...
have you thought?

Cum and history, sticky bedfellows,
creaking mass, mattress critical.
Pustulant sing a loud unclean
and tuned-in renters whistle.

Absinthe makes the tart glow bronzer.
Laudanum makes y'hoes claw longer.

Ego ain't richness,
it poverties,
ego eight inches,
properties.
Wisdom warms hot spots and around damp corners,
Peelers.

Devil's arse, angel breath,
pillow talk without lube,
Double fucked by twelve-inch tridents, we squeal,
We're all Scratchman's arse!

Those without structure know,
leaning, they tower.
Beyond plot, poetry, signature,
literature's a sex-choked whore.

A Small Poem About Not Being

I'll be never enough because hope got there first,
whupped my pert ass 'n' smart-slapped.

Been writing life, was a pesky kid
and far more boysy than led to believe.

They said I was like a girl.
Sometimes sneered it,
making me wear it, bad drag.

Like a girl, nearly died,
scalded my shoulder,
saw too much older and never told.

Been writing death, its brutal alterations;
time knows death,
kissin' cousins twice removed.

You can see me reconfiguring,
reassembling and piecing,
jigsawing a together, forever.
Always doesn't always make always
and solidity's pointless unless you can ride or hug it.

Shadows are only 'not them' when dark,
rest's a reedy romancing, rest runs comically,
rest's side-kick jigging a jaunty theme.

Remembering and forgetting but not forgetting to remember.

I'll be me.

A Small Poem About Anthology

Everything written, forgotten, even unwritten,
are hurriedly scribbled surface hidden,
beyond language and within experience,
we're all anthology.
Human books in world shaped libraries,
I've a million stories,
untold volumes speak louder inside me.
Got books where people used to be,
who are more fond language than prolonged physicality,
one of the complexing meta-gigs of memory.

Been privy to many histories,
their liquoring fogging mystery,
been told of ghosts still living,
making me grieve with necromancing jealousy.
Stories committed to and told,
young, old of biology,
end up in bar-brawled gloops of some wanker's anthology.
But, I'm all othering midnight,
flashing lights and out at sea,
a queen palace'd within half-written uncertainty.
I've a feeling we're all our storage,
battery life and repetitive pouting selfie,
simple snaps of forever competitive technology.

Y'know, there's always been a lighthouse,
a keeper, a rope and an on/off glaring
of vodka on the rocks longevity.

A Small Poem About 'The Poet'

Don't over sing,
leave that same signal too repetitive thing
for those phoney mortgage adverts or Britain's Got Talons.
Imitation's the lesser part of valour,
punch-drunk libertarianism houses fuller hearted candour.

Deliberately moving away from isn't foolish,
it's right,
what art forms deserve.

Skill isn't parodying ventriloquism,
throwing your voice in with the trash water.
It's voice discovery and sound bathing,
blowing soapy grime and bubbling along.

'The Poet' must sit alone,
talk the tall/small with voices making nonsense of spaces
left by other poets able to sit alone.

A Small Poem About Poetry Days

A performance poet's perspective.

Honest smears of word pallets,
sounds splashing purposely fruitful,
so often gloriously accidental.
Intuitively trusting splendour, a must.

Natural and acquired language
and an unquestioning respect for absurdity,
it's not always about understanding.
Knowing glows, but sometimes stops.

Colours running into colours,
sounds into sounds,
words spilling their spin into worlds,
aural drowning.

Lived striations, spittle swirling,
and a literally guttural coming up for air.

A Small Poem About The Unstoppable Crunch

Bones steamroll a pummelling *splat*,
under animated sills of pain, I slide.
Tiny falling an exhausted flat,
hiding within pages of pulp and circumstance.

Think you've read the ending?
Dog-eared futures tumble-weeding.

Where do you stand with the unstoppable crunch?
How do you dodge its poetries?
I've seen Batman's fat cock!
Are comic books stripping down to gaudier levities?

Sometimes think I've written it all,
told everything and spilt,
my cards are stacked a Guinness-stained bookmarked.

Where to start with the unstoppable crunch
and will it ever stop?

A Small Poem About Putting Words In My Mouth

Flesh cage, rattle around, much shape as sound,
shade-tossing in rhythmically ruthless spilling.
Thrilling rooms, splayed spaces,
faces are traces played on open-minded why glides.
Outside's inside, the spitting of pictures,
riches, letter-shaped witches,
spellbound draped on ancient scriptures,
screeching bitches and computer screens.
Purity oddly obscenes, car crashing chaotic serenes,
flesh machines can good man,
they do, they can, flesh machines aren't just bad bullets,
slow decaying, sad delaying,
flesh machines
are chug plod, whirr sting, here 'n' staying.
Never forget playing, cheeky tricking,
the magicking flicking 'n' traipsing of trysts,
slight handling of majestic flurry, strong charms, limp writs,
hubbling bubbling, slow, glazed, blurring mists.
All about haze me;
enthralled by phased days given over to repetitive forgetting.
Regretting works, heartstrings 'n' overtures,
my life's mine, my life's yours, open doors slip-sliding.
We're all divining the dipping, diving,
gliding our own business,
soul-mining word breezes,
tucked into shared intricacies of life's forever
increasing/decreasing creases, and amazing;
well c'mon now, it never fuckin' ceases.
Wizards, screechers,
features, creatures,
leeches, preachers,
knob'eads, teachers.

A Small Poem About Chloe Poems

Clarity of lyrical decibel,
cynical beat-vaudevillian Jezebel
sing-song rhyming a symbiotic ding-dong,
clapped out on ovation's roar and Class-A chemical.
A gingham blur, a routined belle,
she/him, them/they're, Ben her,
been flare gay scene and done it.

Hit 'n' thump with a chequered glove,
boxing in diamanté 'hate/love',
universal rent boy and pub slag,
a bouffant of bobbed riah in her drag bag,
free versed on pulled, sacked, cancelled or fired.

The new rock 'n' roll, frock 'n' dole,
shock 'n' prole, schlock 'n' soul,
gave good as she got but never got the goods back,
inspired.
Anti flag, flew flack 'n' pro craic,
full-on fierce tart attack!

Led with some front, wide eye-liner'd 'n' buoyant,
didn't have a cunt and never forgot the melody.
A salve for many a malady, out 'n' proud Mary,
generous narcissist, artifice leery,
confident outsider, Guinness 'n' cider,
a crisis cross-dressing, eloquently cussing,
triumphantly poetic parody.

A Small Poem About A Little Splash

Avalanching fall-scapes and collects,
languid languaging all boiled up comes stuttering down.
Sometimes I go for it and properly Liverpool swear.

Words are world blind and fighting for recognition.
Words are way over there and without instruction,
institution.
Feel words tiny spatterin' y'eye,
pitter-prattlin' y'mouth.
If spittin' stones,
honey, you'd be pebble-dashin' an alphabet right now.

In stop/starting flurries
it happens, hot-hearting and cold-headed.
Within iced blue lines, white.
If the foolscap tilts,
write it.

A Small Poem About Tories

Robotically talking trust,
Sunak's monosyllabic timbre waters a tinny trickle.
He's mandroid smirking at credibility-strained,
celebrity-drained, sponge blobs.

Penny's dropping her morgue smile,
stench of death semi circles.
Reaper's running, gunning for kids,
rictus-grinning grim rings round truth.
Terminally boring,
but power needs listening to.

Dislike watching pain dry,
greed magnolia splattered over thousand-pound rollers.
I suspect on five-hundred-dollar pizza
they drizzle a light balsamic gold leaf.

Tories may be reading this.
If you are,
you're murderers.

A Small Poem About Boris Johnson

A touch, feeling like burnt lace,
crumpled ashen to ash'd pieces of hate.
I try hard, honestly,
but gave up on rose-tinted spectacle some time ago.
I can on flippant occasion Vaseline smear
a slightly more smudging affair than absolute party.

Watching war unfold
while our clown Premier robes a Ken Dodd pillock.
Apparently he's supporting the people his oligarchs
viscously ripped off.
"Profoundly onside with Britain!"
They're applauding him and I'm told this isn't the end.

Gotta say, never observed it so over,
certainly the last of something.
A different kind of blasphemy;
he's a bulky look of that skinny kid from *The Omen*.

So often told to keep it light,
been intimated I get too heavy.
But after so long witnessing
it would be ungenerous to not document the entropy.

A Small Poem About Liz Truss

Fart cushion with boundary issues,
whoopie blowing a Premier stunk.
Get ready for our wealthy flush to do one,
leave the sunk ship, stinking.

Pork and cheese a flatulent mix,
spatula by golly wow.
Momentarily throne'd heaving big jobbie,
Paisley, so much to answer for.

One of Michael Bentine's Potties gone rogue,
untimely trained for the kill.

A Small Poem About Sociopathy

On some inconceivable level
the whole human race must be collectively sociopathic,
because if not collectively sociopathic
it would've long stopped those incredibly powerful sociopaths
continually leading us into apocalyptic degradations
of poverty and war.

Unless we spell patriotism
I.N.S.A.N.I.T.Y.
I'm lost for words.

A Small Poem About Uncaring

Given up on drain-downed,
swilling around waste of the wasted.
You see them just-eighteen and fifties-quaffed,
sometimes smack-hooked in prams.

No film can capture, no book nor play,
no poem can ever more say.
All our stains never knowing,
never honestly intellectually hoping,
everybody's too busy career validating.
Art is dead!

We won't understand if refusing to understand,
we can't turn running water into diamonds.

Problem is,
I'm petty sure we know we can't drink diamonds.

A Small Poem About Blessed

Not feeling blessed nor reaching spiritual completion,
prayer hasn't paved a clear way or chosen a path,
just crumpled-broken, like the aged can be.
Wrong foot of the crucifix, kiss-less benediction,
signed off the cross, some might say I nailed it.

We're not blessed,
the world's fuckin' pot-holed,
fallen,
godforsaken ankle-torn,
twisted,
bone-bent and splintered.
Cracked!

Not blessed, nor watered holy,
ashen,
just a dirt-daubed forehead and muddy-thumbed rosary.
Priest criss-crosses, bellows, challenges,
and as if by magic suddenly no Purgatory,
so why Heaven and where exactly's Hell?

So blessed are you,
outside of inside and none of the above touches?

A Small Poem About Collapse

Not even a titanium umbrella,
if rain can pass through will protect you.
Ice then slice.

Hitchcock slashes, sound men stabbing,
scythe matters,
breakdown men up-hung swinging.
Hopelessness maddens.

Consequences hit and solution's lost solace.
Bourbon sogging on saucer blocks out willow's bloom.

A Small Poem About Bad Days

My country's dug in its nine-inch nails,
slamming us with face-palmed, napalmed, trajectories.
Poor men slaughtered for being poor,
falling further than fallen, further than thud,
noose hung tall to the floor.
A muddied/sullied further than ever before.

We are blood-bag, bone-sore rejected,
body shamed and left to forage
in half-dreamt grots of Socialism.
Guts of our forefathers' wrench,
bodies turning in graves undug.
Sixpence wages garbage,
insult.

Making tax havens Hell,
faking groundswell support,
taking thunder from applause and darkening skies.
Up there, truth shifts 'n' shapes,
claw-croaks,
roars,
lies.

We are bleak-pit sodden and joyously rotting to the core.

A Small Poem About 'Them'

'They' have it all; Crete's a flippant card tap away,
when it comes to crystalline alternate therapy
just another light-handed pat,
plastic's where it's always been a thumping, bumping,
beat competitive at.
Everything everywhere's theirs,
like they fiscally own rose quartz mines and sunshine.

Festival heart fingers don't boom,
those flesh/bone holes are where souls slip through.
Believe me, if magic were an answer
how could there ever have been famine?

Some twat's hot foie gras-ing some bird's liver,
while some bird picks up a food parcel:
a cold parcel because she hasn't any leccy.

A Small Poem About Flat Earthers

Flat, has to be,
otherwise what other reasons are there?
We have to water, food, shelter, air,
no secrets kept here,
just in y'face, everyday, common/garden need.

Global sounds a too-engaging round
and an over-effulgent, heart-pounding, freed.
Flat grinds a bare-knuckle kneading,
continually bruised, dough-thinning greed.

Out of the two they're not global,
nor a spherically rotund searingly able,
more a just-splattered, broken-boned nosebleed.
They're not about how to reach out,
join hands,
more the fiscally bland, fat-cat-lining,
marginalising profiteering slices of succeed.

Yeah, I know Earth's a sphere,
hear when I say
ain't got no political beef with any of that,
but earthers, man,
too many of those fuckers are so seriously flat.

A Small Poem About Still Not Rising

With all the crucified,
dead 'n' died,
left scraping on the scrapheap
and still we don't rise.

Still don't hug Barabbas,
still isolate Lazarus,
still the hate of survivors
and love of privatisers.

Easter Bunny's a sociopath,
black hole chocolate buttons for eyes;
Easter Bunny's got us all by the balls
and still we don't rise.

A Small Poem About Big World

Big world, you bore me with your car-crashing,
trash-jazzing, pile-highing, Bitcoin agency.
Not only tuneless, clueless, but unintelligibly ruthless.
What bores me more you know and dine out on,
giving you monsoon reasons to bad dance.

Hate big world choosing dance bad
to a rhythmless untrue red, white 'n' blue.

Big world, fuck off, crawl under, seep through,
below pavement disappear.
Every black hole's home for you crater-face,
every water-failing drain 'n' sewer.

Won't get sadder.
Big world, I won't let you win.

A Small Poem About Soils Of Bones

Revelation poor cousins' reality,
balm after storms.
Epiphanies trick half-hearted sanity,
psalm predicting swarms

It's what we've always known, isn't it,
don't answers jest mystically there?
A be-knelt,
no rent crone woman, violently scrubbing stairs.
Prayers,
questions unanswered on garrotted lines.
God,
an unseen spiv with a thirty-piece silvered spine.

What's mine's mine, what's mine's mine!

Emancipation poor relatives' souls,
lost family 'n' friends.
Trends digital, never end,
mazes unavailable on soils of bones.

A Small Poem About Whatever

Gnawing paper-boned musings of ossein-hollered chomps,
what's easily chewed's easier spat out.
Print on my teeth spells smiff-esgtrefkkerropt,
tastes a lot better than reads;
like most things misspelt, a tangibly imagined smudged.

Music's too new,
so I'm top of my tower block ignoring.
Used to sit uncomfortably basement-bound,
passionately miming.

I'd get the lift but it whines discordant,
fucks with whatever's the tune.
Yeah, monoliths sing,
tall songs, small songs, some as big as the led.

You know the words,
blood alliteration of mouth,
little lyrics spittle-written on split lips.

A Small Poem About Ten Times The Size

When you get your tiny on,
everything everywhere's ten times the size.
The towering apocalyptic giant of war,
its profoundly affecting hopelessness,
and you're nothing more than a fractiously,
key-tapping, social media, hapless sunk.
When all around's ten times the size,
you're shrunk.

That over-smiling influencer, dick'ead,
selling tattered Positivia to too-battered teens.
If shelled, he'd probably feel blessed,
humbled, and thank Russia for the inspirational opportunity
of being blown to smithereens.
Gleefully spilling how much he's grown as a man
now splattered up the wall, still smiling,
once in a lifetime inspired by divine synchronicity,
and how being exploded has actually reduced the destructive roar
of his once raging, out of all control, toxic masculinity.

Then pointing you to like, comment, subscribe
to the money sleeking beg of his Patreon.
Maybe selfish egos are ten times the size of war.
For further notifications please twat that bell-end icon.

There's a tonne of things capsizing,
a slew of events colliding,
everything's ten times the size
and that influencer tool's still inanely smiling.

A Small Poem About The Internet

We're none of us atheists because belief's gone digital,
up there in The Cloud our faithlessness and dick pics.

Now we're Our Father who arse and art penis-shaped.
Our presence, our place, our Hell's Heavens
and so many devoted followers.

Talk to people I don't know, they secret speak,
ask me and I answer.
Look down upon the world and the planet's mine to spin.
Mass hysteria critical, a tip-tapping touch away.

Of course we're no longer atheists,
how can we be when too busy aping gods?

A Small Poem About My Understanding Head

Mud-blending and looking for colour,
thick gunge with a rainbow fix,
the bright red I am runs.
Here, have my popper'd-up party lungs
and a body full of heart-deadening plastics.

Remembering dream-flight,
arc-swing, plummet-dipping,
ballsy-winged and coughing up cloud.
Giving birds a paradise for my sunny,
a long gone featherless.

Whirling a blur, keeping up with the dervishes,
on first curse blames with God and spinning out rhythm,
immersive.

Gods used to look like me and I looked like gods.

Pouring it over the floor,
been here, safe.
When saying atheist,
leave this bit out.

There used to be candyfloss, now bollards and spikes,
slow the maelstrom stings.
I'm bled dry, liquating crimson puddles
heat-kilned from blood.

A Small Poem About Heaven

Was sold peace at discount prices,
carved out pearly steps 'n' chiselled cherub wings.
Fairytale breadcrumbs and corner shops, escape.

Statues kind-smirk a smile benign.
How loving lies in crescendo.
How comfort sags through reach.
Twitch me a resting peace stitching my lips 'n' eyes.

Blurring through whispering slits
when screeching though walls.
Giving apostles a Lazarus for their thirty,
commonplace.

Just li'l ol' me mimicking agonised moans,
accompanying life's jagged ascensions.

A Small Poem About Hell

When reaching Hell may I have techno, pills 'n' speed?
Let light run like nymphs neon-phasing through torch song,
a rave of loveless laments helium-squealing.
Cabaret me with demons choralling,
balladeering loathing,
rhythms off-beating are multi-tracked in wicked time.

At wrought irony gates show me pain.
Gift pits burning agony
and skin brand scar with scorched steel acrimony.

Because when finding Hell I'll show you Heaven.

A Small Poem About Satan

My mind's eye had you pin-upped
near The Osmonds, The Rollers and David Essex.
Wanted you ugly next door to pretty,
wanted your grotesque to shine.
Poster boy for the downtrodden and raging,
pride of place, deadly sinning.

Thumbing my brother's Wheatley
and picking out the beast bits,
vivid as Jesus but fired on the other side.
I knew you turned over, what that meant,
lived forever like the bottom bitch you were,
lived forever with your just-fucked tail in the air.

Gave up on hope of forgiveness when like you realised
it guiltily spun on forensic deceptions of apology.

A Small Poem About The Smack Of God

Remember it hitting,
titanic overwhelms tidal-striking.
A kicking punching of instruction,
soundless, clattering, bullying thwacks.

Instinctively understood marvelling,
felt forever stood back,
awe becoming a sense like hearing.
Loved silently listening to awe.

Crowded by prayer and sharing a palace,
flocked by well hung electra-celestials
from whose wings I daily swung.

A Small Poem About Angels

Bliss tricks,
slips in a half kiss and sticks.
You know it, mixed,
spun out 'n' wound up,
candyfloss lip-licked.
Intricate whizzed,
don't wanna jinx or minx it
to busy blow-trumpeting thigh kicks.

Moments, jig high,
lights firing on an all-cylinder super-fly,
wilds in adult and in child, testifies.
We're grounded but when exploding,
we sky.

Spinning in spiralling Wi-Fi,
skyscraper talling bonsai.
In dark books it bright whys,
moments spell, moments mystify.

Always on my ledge, atop and peering.
Anyone down there need a halo?

A Small Poem About The Need To Protect

On an island of pebbles among archipelagos of sand,
sea of acid surrounded, here lies the slight of me.
A slither of self-loathing, bound, tied,
burnt by sun, scarred by moon,
pockmarked-starred and twice-a-day drowning.

Until we big die, we keep small dying,
all that letting go of who, why, however;
we're bad deeds crippled with a panicked need to protect.
We hold ourselves because no one else can,
cage, cradle-wrap.
I'd rock more but far too self-conscious.

Lost 'n' hollow are knotted weights around legs of birds
hopping in frustration at clouds straining to rain.
Some days we realise the world doesn't want us to fly.
We've ousted argument;
it went Bourgeois Zeitgeist passive/aggressive
along with art and listening.
Debate stopped being important and every fucker's right.

I'd deal with the Devil but that shit's no realer than God.
Anybody out there wanna buy a used soul?
Million smiles on the cock and one hell of a careless diver.

A Small Poem About Purity

When people talk of innocence
I just stop.
Whatever it is I'm doing,
stop.

Thinking sinks, doesn't it,
and I don't think ever stops sinking.
Absolutely no idea where it lands.
Perhaps thinking thinks landing's passé.

Makes me feel monochrome lost,
a black/white repetitive ancient.
I've always been a strobing on/off old.

Was told older isn't innocent,
not about purity;
older has blinkered secrets, less security.
The more wrinkles, more dribbling infirm,
more litany of tale-untold impurity.

That's bollocks that though, isn't it?
So tell me, how old are we when first seeing the dark?

That's bollocks as well, isn't it?
Oh fuck it, perhaps everything's bollocks!

A Small Poem About Imagining

Letting them in,
footsteps furred 'n' plodding,
on floorboards talons clack,
in carpet they claw-sink.

Dream them bad on good nights,
on bad nights dream them alone.
Love how shadows scare,
how they monster in movies,
way they're buried in graveyards.

Ivy tangles, green robe,
grub eggs, shell pearl,
nature's imagined jewels.
Fireflies twinkle in animal eyes,
humans forever envy,
fire beasts walk on ice.

Darkness in dawn and dawn darkens.
Fox in bush, rushes,
burn blur brush of rusting dusks,
gone.

This morning, humans jealous of other humans
are talking shop and taking stock.

A Small Poem About Shadowless Excuses

Carnage ashens, arson flakes,
fire-feathers quill-scorch horizons.
That place memories mirage and nobody's there,
none of us are present in our pasts or futures.
The olfactory seasonality of burnt offerings.

Hollowing amber,
traps in ointments ills,
our salves homemade, blister.
Skin covered cottons,
soft as synthetic.
The hives 'n' the hive nots riot
and our itched-inflamed scorch on.

I keep cursing words too said,
not said enough,
shadowless excuses muted, muffled.
Without information,
whispers colourless, land.

In other deserts, other dawns,
hot cold, ancient,
sat around fire the same old stories,
just torn meat and reasons.

A Small Poem About Expectation

Often wonder if I've genuinely had any,
can't top-of-my-head think.
Must have though, surely we all do,
but too much was taken from me to confidently trust time.

Been accused of not taking career seriously,
they were dead on,
there was never another day, never mind decade.
Tomorrow's a rickety rusting set of traps,
half-cocked 'n' cooked, ready to ankle-snap.

Didn't get to call the future,
we were never that close.
Too busy romancing impossibility to truly care
for anything remotely approaching expectation.

A Small Poem About Reaching

From my solar plexus an invisible arm grabs,
knows something's not there,
but could, should, and might have always been.
Isn't but is my arm, a third forever straining.

Doing it now, clawing,
weaving through chest and ribs.
Can't want it,
but cherish its need.

I'm human-alien,
detailed scribbled by troubled artists,
lead embedded in surrealist sci-fi fever-scheming.

Not a leg or head, an arm almost escaping.
I think it knows what isn't.
Wiser than my other arms,
reaching.
Sometimes feel edge of its shoulder,
perhaps more.
Fuckin' 'ell, are there other me's in 'ere?

On its skin,
arrow-speared and ribbons billowing,
a tattooed bloodied heart.
Inked knuckles punch,
y·e·a·r·n and s·o·r·r·o.

A Small Poem About Depression

Like you've never known yourself,
yet comes with so much of yourself,
like you've always known 'n' never known you.

With me it creaks, old doors nowhere-ing,
pointless compasses of no-when,
no physicality,
reflectionless crowds of the mirrored gone.
Parties without guests,
without party,
no invite.

You know it's coming;
thudding, shuddering, stomp of giant's steps,
but where's the fucking giant?
What's the point of fairytale protagonists
with little or no story?
The arrogant hopelessness of nameless Goliaths.

Gnaws rat-like underneath ribs,
claws pulsating in cauldron-plops of stomach.

With me, it creaks.

A Small Poem About Anxiety

Lives in my stomach
an electric punch and flesh itch,
bubbles, retching out for further corruption.

Gives me a limp, a stutter, worms;
if human it would be a breathless dog.
A yappy unhappening dog, snapping and unloveable,
scraping its shitty hoop along a grassy knoll.
Kind of dog you'd gladly put out of your misery.

Ugly powerful, a hard cackling supervillain,
stretch-sketched in untouchable evil.
It and my insomnia crack jokes about puny humans
and world domination.

Have it like attack and snarl,
it would happily bite a baby.
Have it like companion,
the one planning my murder.

Someone once pointed me to mindfulness
and chamomile tea…
they're lucky I didn't glass 'em.

A Small Poem About The Rattle

Because can't see future
liken it to not being able,
why I have to make do with a cracking now.
Explains my love for the past,
can remould it,
old/young it, coward/bold it.
Lives known, freeing,
word clay splattered onto Potter's wheeling.

So, unable to future,
that special peace taken from me.
Horror of The Rattle crackles ceaselessly pithily.

The Rattle snake oils freedom,
shreds skin seweraging,
ages, debases.
The Rattle starts in childhood's marrow,
vibrating in between loss 'n' sorrow,
races yesterday's losing to tomorrow.
The Rattle close-chest holds the spaded aces.

Drinking trumpets a blurred escaping,
The Rattle rapping scoffs at sleeping,
nightmares dart, skin piercing.
I'm out 'n' out, in 'n' in, out 'n' in,
watching lots of puppy videos and shrinking.

A Small Poem About Being Mean

If chaos is all you've known, all you'll know is chaos.
Might not be battering your head right now,
but just one sharp corner,
a too-quick spin even, and what's gone *boom*, falls out.

We are mean and don't understand chaos.
Throw it out windows like it can bluebird away and melody.
Frightened of frailty and wing are why we don't fly.
We are mean and don't understand, Garland knows.

Anxious cradling of heavy hearts.
Swung low of sweetless chariots and deep-earthed
we decay in long-played out accountancies of greed.
It's how we forged bridges, dug canals, chiselled song.
Perhaps we're always graved,
always greedy,
always chaos.

I've been mean and not understood,
deliberately, to make life go away.
But if chaos is all you've known, all you'll know is chaos.

A Small Poem About Nightmares

Plagued by my beloved resurrected,
under nails their flesh,
pink skins of relationship are blood-torn and zombie.

Middle of explosion and breaking everywhere,
four corners directionless and eviscerated.

Clawing escape for desperate of awake,
fangs dig, hard bones crack 'n' splinter.
Grabbing at sky terrors and missing.

Sunsets of suffocate,
smother mouth and cover nose,
sulphur breaths of threatening pillow.

A Small Poem About Waking Up

Littered noise,
embittered sound,
jittered jolts 'n' juddering.
Bad-dreamt shuddering and glooped-eyed,
alert surprise at paralysis sleeping.

Waking ain't easy,
but someone's gotta to do it.

A Small Poem About Door

Inspired by a Stephen Cassidy painting.

I'm a massive portal 'ead,
spaces lurking within spaces, rock my world.
Tiny frames doors take up, fascinate,
a no-one's land or places for everybody.
Get frisson'd-up to fuck sometimes,
neck electric, just stepping across,
that's all it takes.

Not the only one, never been an only one.
One shade in a long line of shades just passing through.

Once in Ireland, rural Ireland,
I spied a deserted house, its blue door,
brilliant blue and somewhat anachronistic.
Big time wanted in but it wouldn't let me.
This wasn't my house, my door,
not welcome, not allowed.

An old friend's painted a door of oceans unseen.
Deeps of cautionary wheres,
seeps of somewheres here, over there 'n' in-between...
behind closed,
screams.

Once told a mate doors possessed mystery.
Laughing out loud, told me I was wrong, stupid.
He was shut off to doors, closed,
wrong, stupid.

A Small Poem About Longevity

There's a door near a door very near another door.
Knock knock!
Who's there?
Your future.
My future, what?

Can't see tomorrow,
today's always misty,
making yesterday's weather a fogging sunny.
See, that's it with calendared certainty,
stormy.

Put a just-found shell to your ear and what do you hear?
Knock knock!
Who's there?
Your future.
My future, how?

See, that's it with calendared certainty,
stormy.

A Small Poem About Uncertainty

When life's signposted a particular way
I've historically walked another.
Little interest in certainty,
ask anybody who knows me, really knows,
never seriously courted the cosier thralls of security.

Mine a quirkily haphazard gait,
made from theatre, rave, nuance, mince and Mersey,
walking my way certainly puckered it pout of me.

Sometimes the signpost vanishes,
stolen by a sticky-fingered, too-long wintered,
infernally-embittered fate.
Wherever it finishes, however it starts,
sometimes that bastard'n signpost's
driven straight through y'broke, bleedin' heart.

A Small Poem About Task

Overwhelming/celebrating it consumes,
conjures and dictates.
Shivering within/without recollection,
lingers on in outlines.

Companions and when alone, labours,
a wronging road weighted by phantom event
I'm at loss to identify or make manifest.
So meander down meaningless,
bumbling along on longing founds of direction.

Confronted with bludgeoning punchlines,
and everybody's ringside waiting for the knockout.
Sprawl-splattered on bloodied canvas,
my cheek.

I'm 'The Artwork', avant-surrealist daubed,
crumpled-drunk, pitiful-weft and dancing.
Tasked by weights of collision and falling family.

Ring a ring o' narcissists, pockets full o' why.
People tell me I've words.
I've only words because I've life,
tasking.

Still do cute, often have too, sometimes cute's all I've got.

Today's task, recognise task,
gift it form, magic, tragedy and of course, words.

A Small Poem About Where I'm Not

Sat here still reaching and kinda leaning out myself,
a spooky rectangular intangible,
more Mrs Muir than ghost but always ghost.
An outside-of-bodied experience,
halted by faithlessness.
Listen dick'ead, if belief could make career happen
it would have happened long before now.

I'm onside with the losers,
like their take,
cynicism rocks.
Rage is honester than politeness and angry knows joy.
Pretty certain our too-content can't dance.

So I'm not here un-sat with myself,
no longer pass 'n' parcelling time.
Stopped raging when boredom clawed in
and in a relationship with a me who isn't,
who wouldn't have chosen this.

Not sure I fancy or even like myself anymore.

A Small Poem About Making Sense Of Directionless

No tears, not yet,
North, East, West, South.
Morals compassed,
NEWS flashing, weathered,
vain's a cardinal seen.

You don't know where,
spun,
whirling around, rusty,
cocks of the walk, limping,
making sense of directionless.

Four points for seven bothers.
There were brides,
wild nights and ale house parties.
I brought home my weekly wishing.

Creaks, time,
a monochromatic Technicolor'd,
wound-up blurring and howling.
I'm pointing here, it's pointing there,
time's fuckin' pointin' every-fuckin'-where.

We're stuck
'til somewhere else,
a nowhere where we're gone.

Paradise points to unending heavenlessness.

A Small Poem About Powerlessness

Fear monsters,
gargantuan-mouthed and razor sharp.
From flesh roaring caverns emptying bowels of blame.

Stuck, and cracks are reverberating,
tectonic plate earthquaking.
Get a move on, everywhere's a stumbling stagger,
beyond wibbly-wobbling and not falling down,
we're Weeble-ing.

Forgettable, grits between rubbling stones,
long-unsung songs, door-to-door sung by tremor.

That howling light,
slowly disappearing,
fogging out into eternal pitch of fright noise.

A Small Poem About Suicidal Ideation

A lake, some stillness and balmy breezes,
when quiet dominates, it dominates,
even green, it's metropolis silent.
Don't trust noiselessness,
it pointy-finger beckons.

There's a lost of somewheres,
they shady everywhere,
street signs scrawled with your name on.
Some somewheres don't have your name on,
some somewheres promised to but never did.

It's a black shit of space,
cluttered with a dumped-off unseen.
Boris Johnson's in there,
bottom of the pile, top of his game.

A Small Poem About Beyond

I'm attracted to cliff edges,
they scare me and looking down, panics.
Do them though, go far as I dare and I dare.
Head rush confuses, elates,
not spun enough to fall but isn't out the question.

Questions, vision distant and dizzy blur,
they're beyond imaging composition.
Not making sense, invites,
I'm at home with furniture rearranges,
pictures fall, frames shatter,
dig torn photography and broken glass.

Consider height, compliments toppling,
It 'n' I history'd.
Wind-thrashed and breath-taken,
then wonder where it goes.
Are breaths taken immortal whispers
partying with other breaths taken run out of things to say?

One foot fronts the other, tippy-toe'd inching excites.
Attrition chips at and chalks of cliff edge tumble.
Land of soft soap and tall story!
Candles blow, making three depth wishes.

Sometimes sing what I can't recall.
Always the right song though,
themed to situation.

A Small Poem About Aimed And Internally Dangerous

Sights pinpointed are noir silhouetted,
head's a disappointed battered.

Paint another's corpse round my body,
broken,
targeted,
chalk-outlined,
splattered,
think I'm linked to the Kennedys.

Disfigured and weight, disinfected and late,
disingenuous hate,
dead wait, a shut gate worried.

Bone buried in backyards paved,
crazy-graved 'n' petal-dashed,
tears splash crocodile in soft-shoe handbags.
Lost glad-rags bespoken,
shrouded, token,
dead don't speak until unspoken.
In back rooms crowded misery,
in history pokin',
dead are smokin'.

Flaunting,
you bring out the death in me,
haunting.

A Small Poem About Nowhere

Is that?
Was that?
Are we?

A Small Poem About Shadows

Shadows, how they near own you,
wrap without arms,
hug without held,
how deep within depth they disown you.

Gripping dramas of darkening curtain,
gotta hand it to them,
if loving you, fuck man, they love you.

I know names,
sly as silk making you shadow.
I've passed through walls not there,
shut-eye glimpsing half-arsed love.

Ever kissed shadows,
swallowed their hollow tongues?
I shark-heart the shady caress of whisper.

Home in blackness,
and shadows familial gather.
Their's a crowding hierarchy,
but they won't let you see.

A Small Poem About Struggle

Ancient chains and eternal worry,
there are race memories somewhere with our shame on.

I blame the grandparents of parents of parents
forced into marriage unable to read or write.
I blame the peoples with nothing,
historical losers on prehistoric Jeremy Kyle,
I blame the victim!
I blame that spotty, lazy, sabre-toothed skiver on benefits.

I blame slum dwellers rotten with dysentery and pleurisy,
as for rickets, I blame that too.
I blame mothers for infant mortality,
all they had to do was pull down their skirts,
close their legs and open *The Bible*.
I blame the blamed because they blame themselves
for every time poverty made them fail.
Blame them for being poor.
Blame them for monkey pox, no more white dog poo,
rubella, polio and measles.

Aching frames us and we're forever sorry;
there's debased beggary somewhere with our blame on.

A Small Poem About Catastrophising

Flopping flip of a letter box and needle-piercing,
flesh-pinching stabs of my ringtone
put childhood memories of Christopher Lee to shame.
It's always, if I look to my door,
pick up my phone…
what?

Nine times out of ten of course it's Heaven not Hell,
but equations can't be trusted.
Part of me hates Numbers,
because part of me always knew she didn't add up.
It's why I like Sundays, because everybody's off.
Six from seven leaves one.

Pull yourself together… they so often say…
You're making monsters out of mole hills…
but this shit's scarier than Dracula.

A Small Poem About Time

Written the morning of John Grimes's funeral.

Morning's powerfully invisible, divisible within bygone.
Time's done and shadow passing over bridges
our gang's a brand new ghost.
Old Father and I have never properly got on.

Lonely of it, body-centred and soul-stretching,
wretched getting in the pull.
Time culls and hungover mulls in goodbye a final
night night.

Dreamt Heaven but long stopped believing.
Time spent grieving, time spent waiting,
time ding-dinging never misses last buses
forever leaving.

Time, where does it go?
Time fast, time slow?
Time, yes, time, no.

A Small Poem About The Last Lap

Water's weaving an eternal parentless,
tonight, sea's coloured careless and a cloying playless.
Full of life's after, oceans are wholly prayerless.
Behind tears our sureless wash up.

How do you cuddle the dead,
how do we make it right for them,
another forehead kiss 'n' *night night*?
C'mon now, how does any of this make sense?

The marina's whispering then screams out
dreams undreamt.
Seashells unkempt, too sandy for ears,
too-near fears whisper-trickle your face.

Big man's tall before picking you up;
who knows, could be you all grown.
Sounds of sure, shore small.

A Small Poem About Grief

First footprints, long stepped,
first swim, long swam,
nobody recalls their first crawl.

Our walled-in wails though,
those silences,
loud as garlanded deities awaiting prayer.
Love makes us God-sized,
loss bigger.

Nothing yet everything.

A sky of gone.

From little tears mighty egos grow.

A Small Poem About Loss

They un-live an imagined next door,
empty house, furnished by un-happened.
Moved to furthest reaches of the outskirts some time ago.

I'm not alone in isolation,
we all experience this.
Of course I've poems,
maybe too many.

Those impossible distances,
often written, not truly captured.
Always known I haven't right words…
y'know, don't think there are right words.

Pretty sure you can't satisfactorily capture what isn't there.

Sometimes feel it like mist,
half-formed nearly droplets.

A Small Poem About Unseeing

Looking, hardly sees.
Staring out moments,
half-glimpsed gloom spies a blur.
At best, I bet looking guesses.

Look sometimes and am still,
frame-frozen but not cold,
just hardly seen or seeing.
It's always a cliff-edged 'what if'
in front of my eyes.

When spied, sometimes hardly there,
I'm somewhere else with our frisky unseeable.
The once unmissable are still missing.

I prefer glare of flare-blinding suns.
So bright,
so nothing and left unseeing.

A Small Poem About Being Right Twice A Day

Probably over the cognitive understanding thing.
Finished hurtling into chaotic malleability.

Not saying I'm right,
not saying I'm skilled,
more can't say anymore
and all my imagined invisibility's gone.

Not sociopathic, not uninvolved,
stopped.

A clock not wanting wound.
Cloth ears not wanting sound.
Unloved lost property not wanting found.

Stopped.

A Small Poem About Disassociation

When a kid I had a spaceship,
it took me from emotion to an outer place,
wider the vista, smaller the world.
An off-planet happier,
no aliens or lifeforms,
nothing to love or lose.

Skimming supernovas is a serious skill,
convinced myself I was the only one.
Thousands of us out there,
other spaceships piloted invisible,
black-inking in sci-fi jams of stars-twinkling escape.

When grown up you let go of the ship
but never the space.

A Small Poem About Space

Nothing's tumbling,
I'm rolling around absent tundra,
there's un-roots un-weeding wildly about.
Nothing in nothing,
in something,
space.

When long gone or newly occupied,
that's the thing with space:
it fills.

Remembering building sandcastles with moats,
intricately detailed, finger-poked turret windows.
Took great care making them impenetrable.

Sea's a bitch!

A Small Poem About Seeing

One night we'll finger-reach a light
so blinding it'll scorch out sight.
Then we'll feel what we're too frightened to see
and read a Braille of stars.

Sized Queens

[a li'l playlet… or is it a big one?]

Scene: *A bright, white-sanded desert-scape, balmy warm, calmly still, with more than a hint of jasmine'd scent and the dreamlike eternal. There may even be chimes. Embedded within all of this, from 1970, Li'l Gerrid [Scouse for Gerard], a mousey, lank-haired, eight-year-old boy, in his hand a Barbie Doll. He's closed-eyed, looking to and bathing in relaxing, throbbing wafts of beating down sunshine. In a sci-fi teleporting all-of-a-suddenly from 2022, Big Gerry 1970s-special-effect appears. He's just turned sixty, there's a baggy tiredness about the eyes and a slightly more round-shouldered gait, but still vitally aware and physically interested in the vast open nature of his new surroundings [or are they?].*

Li'l Gerrid: Remember?

Big Gerry: Yes, our desert. Wow, big isn't it?

Li'l Gerrid: Has to be.

Big Gerry: Oh, I know, still visit from time to time. Although it's always slightly different when you're in it. To be honest, feels a bit crowded.

Li'l Gerrid: I didn't ask you to come 'ere, did I?

Big Gerry: I don't know, did you?

Li'l Gerrid: How do I know? Well, y'ere now, aren't ye!

Big Gerry: Suppose so. In this li'l book of poetry I'm remembering the spaceship more, just beamed down from it now, but completely loved/love it here.

Li'l Gerrid: Yeah, 'avin' you 'ere's a bit funny as well. The spaceship's gear though inni, love flyin' it out the window.

Big Gerry: Zooming out of 6A Blackstock Gardens, hitting the dusking skies of the docks, skimming the slate grey silver of The Mersey, and then soaring into the off/on twinkling oblivion of outer space. The most fun anyone can have with their eyes closed.

Li'l Gerrid: Dick'ead!

Big Gerry: Cheers kid.

Li'l Gerrid: I re-draw'd the spaceship cartoon colours so's it'd be funnier.

Big Gerry: You were drawing, colouring-in and cartoon mad; remember The Fantastic Four?

Li'l Gerrid: Course I do, it was on yesterday, divvy. The Thing said "it's clobberin' time". Love it when he says tha'.

Big Gerry: Seem to remember you loving Susan Storm more, The Invisible Girl.

Li'l Gerrid: Oh yeah, I adore 'er, she's dead fab, but The Thing can smash down walls with one fist and I'd rather be able to do tha' right now than go invisible.

Big Gerry: Why?

Li'l Gerrid: Invisible enough as it is. Don't wanna get more invisible, do I?

Big Gerry: No, you don't.

Li'l Gerrid: They can't 'elp it though.

Big Gerry: Can't help what?

Li'l Gerrid: Not seein' me.

Big Gerry: What's going on outside of here?

Li'l Gerrid: Our Tommy, he's died as well now, him 'n' Jimmy, gone. It's all goin' mad in the 'ouse, kickin' off bad style.

Big Gerry: I know.

Li'l Gerrid: Everything's grown-up-shaped.

Big Gerry: Hence the desert.

Li'l Gerrid: No one but me.

Big Gerry: Except me.

Li'l Gerrid: You are me, just much bigger.

Big Gerry: But we're both very tiny in here.

Li'l Gerrid: Tiny's good though inni, means y'can hide.

Big Gerry: Get invisible?

Li'l Gerrid: Shurrup kleverclogs.

Big Gerry: Sorry Jelly Beans, don't mean to be, force of habit.

Li'l Gerrid: You sure you're me?

Big Gerry: Yeah, why?

Li'l Gerrid: Y'always sound dead posh 'n' stupid.

Big Gerry: Suppose I do to you, but believe me I don't sound dead posh to dead posh people. I've moved around a bit, tried new things. Was an incredibly well-spoken gay, socialist, transvestite poet and gingham diva for quite some time, so my Scouse voice isn't strong as it once was. Blame Chloe.

Li'l Gerrid: Chloe?

Big Gerry: Certainly not strong as yours, you sound like a high-pitched Fuzzy-Felt, Una Stubbs, Scottie Road, glove puppet.

Li'l Gerrid: What's Fuzzy-Felt, who's Una Stubbs, Chloe who? Eeeee, you don't 'alf sound like a proper poshnob, you do.

Big Gerry: It's just what happens when you grow up and move on, you don't stay or sound the same.

Li'l Gerrid: Does growin' up mean it all goes away?

Big Gerry: No, not all, but sometimes there's valuable comforting distance.

Li'l Gerrid: Oh, like the sound of tha'. T'be 'onest with ye, it's all too close at the mo. Like livin' in the middle of a Vauxhall Road pile up, everythin' keeps crashin' down.

Big Gerry: I remember some but a lot of that stuff's gone, blocked it out, had to. The bit you're going through now with Thomas, most of that's disappeared. There's some memory, flashes of things, I recall the church and funeral.

Li'l Gerrid: Tha' 'asn't 'appened yet. Next week.

Big Gerry: In a funny way, some of that bit's nice; you'll love the story chair and there's other gorge moments, comforting ones. People being incredibly kind and clods of earth spring to mind.

Li'l Gerrid: Things 'aven't bin comfortable for ages now and don't think they're ever gonna be again.

Big Gerry: Can't lie to y'kid, it's gonna be a rough ride.

Li'l Gerrid: Y'don't have to be a big grown up to know tha'.

Big Gerry: No, y'don't.

Li'l Gerrid: Can't wait to be all grown up 'n' big.

Big Gerry: Oh yeah, some of it'll be the best of times. I promise, you'll dance for what seems like forever and no one will enjoy it more than you. Well, except everyone going through their own bonkers life stuff, but some people see the esoteric importance of it more and you deffo will. Esoteric means spooky.

Li'l Gerrid: I love spooky things.

Big Gerry: Then you're gonna love The Shiver; it's a bit like this but with your own wall-less gods, flashing lights and never-ending music. The laughing kid, oh you'll never know hysterics like it. You're gonna meet people who'll completely blow your Captain Scarlet socks off and the endless adventure of it all will make every night a wide-eyed disco happening. No one's really just like anybody else, a daft thing to even suggest, but in fabulously different ways there are people out there dripping in big fabulousness just like fabulous li'l you, and you'll find and love them with all your gingham pinafore'd, Judy Garlanded heart.

Li'l Gerrid: Not arsed about any of tha'. It's just all this inni, there's too much goin' on, an' let me tell ye somethin' fer nottin': no matter how much good life y'keep tryin' to give me from the future you'll never live more life than wha' I'm livin' through right now. It's never gonna get bigger than what's goin' on 'ere.

Big Gerry: *[A stunned, jaw-dropped pause]* Jesus Christ, you're right.

Li'l Gerrid: Are you doin' tha' writin' letter to y'younger self thing? Well, if y'are, don't, cos right now I could write you a Ladybird Bible and throw it right back at ye.

Big Gerry: No Inspirationalism, no Positivia.

Li'l Gerrid: Wha'?

Big Gerry: This is where I learnt it.

Li'l Gerrid: Don't know wha' y'mean.

Big Gerry: I do, or am beginning to.

Li'l Gerrid: More riddles than The Riddler, you.

Big Gerry: Scousers for ye Robin, twenty words when you only need a look.

Li'l Gerrid: Y'know I come 'ere for the quiet, don't ye?

Big Gerry: Yup and I'm spoiling it, aren't I?

Li'l Gerrid: Yeah, y'are actually.

Big Gerry: I'll pop off then.

Li'l Gerrid: Like *I Dream of Jeannie*.

Big Gerry: Exactly like.

Li'l Gerrid: I like the way you do tha', will y'do the nod this time?

Big Gerry: I'll do the nod.

Li'l Gerrid: I like 'er an' *The Ghost an' Mrs Muir*. Love ghosts.

Big Gerry: Well, that's gonna come in well handy.

Li'l Gerrid: An' I wanna dog juss like Scruffy.

Big Gerry: You'll have to make do with Sheba. Or is it Queenie? Think it's Queenie, can never quite remember.

Li'l Gerrid: Kinda wanna be on me own now.

Big Gerry: Alright, I get the hint. I'll leave you to our desert; it is more you than me. I might zhuzh myself back to the future in our spaceship.

Li'l Gerrid: Zhuzh, what's zhuzh?

Big Gerry: What you dream of, Jeannie.

Li'l Gerrid: Oh I like tha'. An' I might see ye in outer space. Don't forget the nod.

Big Gerry: Okay, okay, bloody hell you're impatient. Actually, still are. Seriously like it here, and it's just made me realise another big something.

Li'l Gerrid: What's tha'?

Big Gerry: Why I've always loved feeling dwarfed.

Li'l Gerrid: Y'mad you.

Big Gerry: Something like that. Y'ready?

Li'l Gerrid: Wha' for?

Big Gerry: The li'l nod, y'big divvy.

Li'l Gerrid: Wait a minni!

Big Gerry: What now?

Li'l Gerrid: Do I still colour-in and draw all the time?

Big Gerry: Kind of, but with words, not pictures.

Li'l Gerrid: Knob'ead!

Big Gerry: Do you want this nod or what?

Li'l Gerrid: Oh, go 'ed, then.

Big Gerry crosses his arms over his chest, makes huge, wide eyes, snaps them shut, then vigorously one-nods his head. There's a bright light twinkling sound and he instantly vanishes. Li'l Gerrid's left alone, giggling.

Li'l Gerrid: It's so much more betterer with the nod, makes loads more sense than a silly twitchy nose.

Li'l Gerrid lies back into warm, soft, white sand; he's at peace enjoying the bright calm of the sun. Finally, he's able to think and relax; doesn't even want to play out with his mates, just rest. On slightest of breezes there's a pained distant noise; as it gets louder a gale picks up and begins to storm the desert. Between cloying howl of wind's-wail and skin-stinging stabs of sand, madly blinking, he hears a clearly anguished woman calling out... "Gerrid, where are ye lad, where are ye, I need y'ere with me, this minute!"

Li'l Gerrid: Oh no, it's me Ma callin' me in, wha' does she want wi' me now? I'd berrer get straight back to 6A.

Without as much as a nod, and like he seriously doesn't want to, he slowly, sadly disappears. He's right though, it's so much more betterer with the nod.

The End

(or is it?)